LIVES
AND
TIMES

Louis Braille

Jayne Woodhouse

Heinemann Interactive Library,
Des Plaines, Illinois

Published by Heinemann Interactive Library,
an imprint of Reed Educational & Professional Publishing,
1350 East Touhy Avenue, Suite 240 West
Des Plaines, IL 60018

Produced by Times Offset (M) Sdn. Bhd.
Designed by Ken Vail Graphic Design.
Illustrations by Hemesh Alles

02 01 00 99 98
10 9 8 7 6 5 4 3 2 1

Library of Congress Cataloging-in-Publication Data

Woodhouse, Jayne, 1952–
    Louis Braille/Jayne Woodhouse,
        p. cm. -- (lives and times)
    Includes bibliographical references and index.
    Summary: A simple biography of the man who invented a special system of
raised dots on paper enabling blind people to read.
    ISBN 1-57572-559-2
    1. Braille, Louis, 1809–1852-- Juvenile literature. 2. Blind teachers -- France --
Biography -- Juvenile literature. (1. Braille, Louis, 1809–1852. 2. Teachers. 3. Blind.
4. Physically handicapped.) I. Title. II. Series: Lives and times (Crystal Lake, Ill.)
HV1624.B65W66 1997
686.2'82'092 -- dc21
(B)   97-13733
                                                                                  CIP
                                                                                   AC

Some words are shown in bold, **like this**.
You can find out what they mean by looking
in the glossary. The glossary also helps you say
difficult words.

Acknowledgments

The author and publishers are grateful to the following for permission to reproduce copyright
photographs:
Eye Ubiquitous/Paul Seheult, pp.17, 18, 19, 20, 21, 22, 23

Cover photograph: Mary Evans Picture Library

Special thanks to Betty Root for her comments in the preparation of this book.

Every effort has been made to contact copyright holders of any material reproduced in this
book. Any omissions will be rectified in subsequent printings if notice is given to the publisher.

Contents

Part One

Do you know how blind people read? They use books written in **braille**. The books have little raised dots instead of letters. The children read with their fingers, not with their eyes.

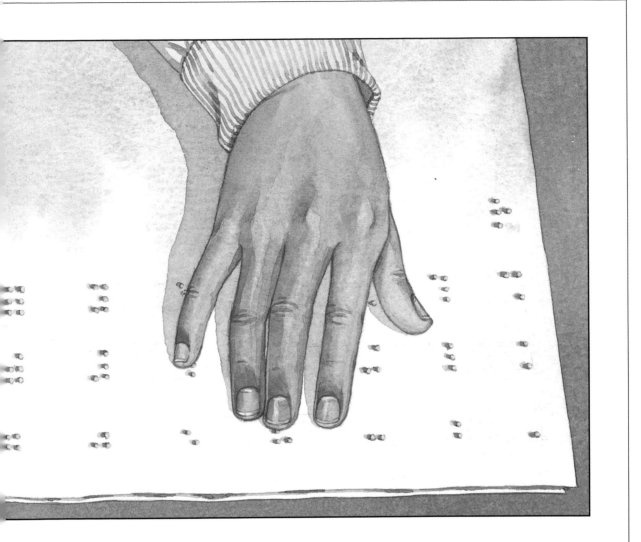

Braille is named after **Louis Braille**, the man who invented this special writing for blind people. This is his story.

Louis Braille was born in France in 1809, nearly 200 years ago. His father was a **saddler**.

When he was a little boy, Louis loved to play in his father's workshop. "Don't touch the knives!" said his father. "They are too sharp for you."

One day, when he was three, Louis picked up a knife. He tried to cut with it. But the knife slipped and went into his eye.

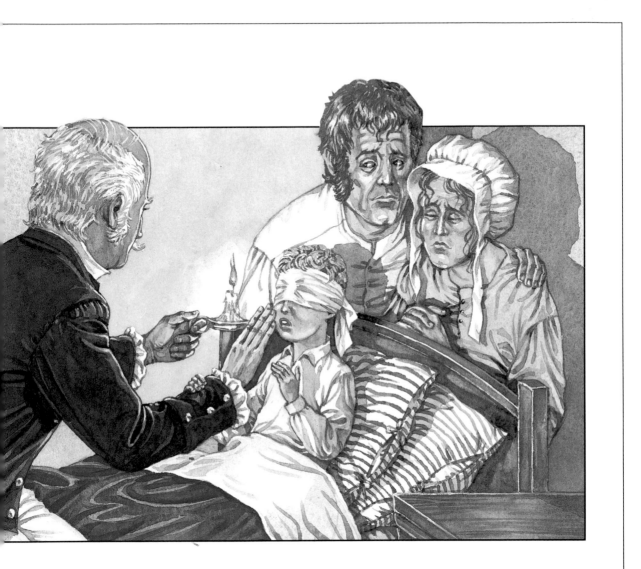

Then his other eye began to hurt, too. The
doctor could not help. Soon Louis could
not see. He was blind.

When Louis was ten, he went to a special school for blind children. It was in **Paris**, a long way away from his home.

Louis learned to read from large books. The letters stood out. He had to feel each letter with his fingers. It was very slow and very hard.

Louis wanted to find a quicker way to read.
When he was only 13, he had a good idea.
"I will change the letters into dots," he said.
"Then they will be easier to feel."

Louis made up different patterns of dots for each letter. He made a special ruler to press the dots into the paper. The dots stuck out so you could feel them. Reading and writing were now much easier.

Louis's school teachers did not like his idea. "You cannot use this here!" they said.

When Louis grew up, he became a teacher at the school. He never forgot his idea. He worked to make it better and better.

Louis was very sad that no one liked his idea for making reading and writing for blind people easier. He was sick for a long time. He died when he was only 43.

A	B	C	D	E	F	G	H	I	J
K	L	M	N	O	P	Q	R	S	T
U	V	X	Y	Z	and	for	of	the	with

W	Oblique stroke	Numeral sign	Poetry sign	Apostrophe sign	Hyphen		
	;	:	.	,	!	( )	? "	"

Not long after he died, people saw that Louis's dots really were a good idea. Today, blind people all over the world use **braille** to read and write.

Part Two

This is a **portrait** of Louis Braille.

It shows you what he looked like.

These are some dominoes that Louis
played with. They are displayed in the
house where Louis was born.

Visitors can go to the house where Louis was born. It is now a **museum**. Inside, you can see some of his family's belongings, like the dominoes.

This is Louis's father's workshop. Look at all the sharp tools. It was here, with one of these tools, that Louis hurt his eye.

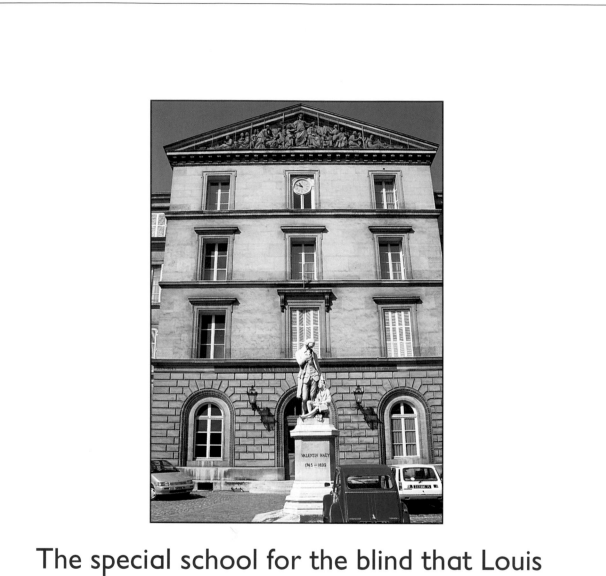

The special school for the blind that Louis attended is still there in **Paris**. Here is a photograph of it today.

If you ever go to Paris, you can visit the **tomb** where Louis Braille is buried. It is in a famous building called the **Panthéon.** The tomb tells you when he died.

Glossary

This glossary explains difficult words, and helps you to say words which may be hard to say.

artifacts things which people make and use are artifacts. We can learn about the past by looking at old artifacts. You say *AR tuh faks*.

Braille These are raised dots on paper blind people use to read and write. You say *brayl*.

Louis Braille you say *LOO ee brayl*.

museum This is a building that has lots of **artifacts** in it.

Panthéon This is a building in Paris that contains the tombs of many famous people. You say *PAN thee ahn*.

Paris Capital city of France.

portrait This is a picture of a person, showing their face.

saddler Person who makes and repairs saddles and leather harnesses for horses.

tomb Where a dead person is buried.

Index

More Books to Read

Davidson, Margaret. *Louis Braille: The Boy Who Invented Books for the Blind.* New York: Scholastic, 1991.